THE WILTS AND BERKS CANAL REVISITED

30 August 2006. Neil Rumbol, the founder of the Wilts & Berks Canal Amenity Group (now WBCT), and Audrey Smith, a former chairperson of the IWA, are seated on the bow of narrowboat *Hakuna Matata* at the official opening of Jubilee Junction.

THE WILTS AND BERKS CANAL REVISITED

DOUG SMALL

The Duchess of Cornwall officially opening Double Bridge, May 2009.

First published 2010

The History Press
The Mill, Brimscombe Port
Stroud, Gloucestershire, GL5 2QG
www.thehistorypress.co.uk

British Library Cataloguing in Publication Data.
A catalogue record for this book is available from the British Library.

ISBN 978 0 7524 5146 6

Typesetting and origination by The History Press
Printed in Great Britain
Manufacturing managed by Jellyfish Print Solutions Ltd

CONTENTS

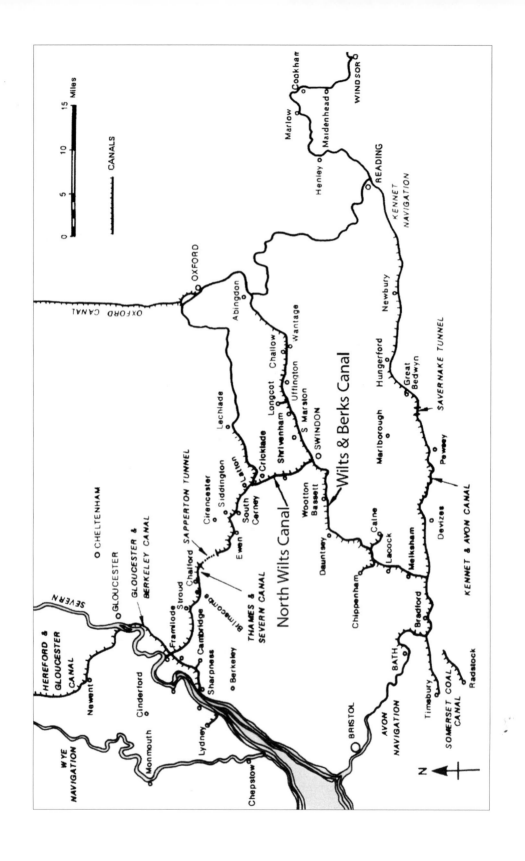

INTRODUCTION

Late in the eighteenth century, in rather a panic at the thought of missing out on the 'Canal Mania' that had been sweeping the country for some years, the Earl of Peterborough together with some of his friends and acquaintances, plus other interested businessmen and landowners, came up with a scheme for a new canal that passed through the Vale of the White Horse. Several routes were surveyed and discarded until, after protracted discussions with the Kennet & Avon Canal Company, a line between Semington, two miles south of Melksham, and Abingdon, on the River Thames, was finally settled upon. The appointed engineers, William and Robert Whitworth, father and son, eventually began the construction at Semington, in preference to Abingdon, thereby allowing coal from the Somersetshire fields to be traded up the new canal as each section of it was completed. As soon as the trade started, much needed revenue would then be generated.

William Whitworth was insistent, in a letter to the Wilts & Berks Canal proprietors, that a regulating stop lock should be built at Semington to prevent the much-valued water resources being lost to the Kennet & Avon Canal. He wrote:

> Here it may be proper to observe that there is absolute necessity to build a Regulating Lock to the Kennet & Avon Canal … otherwise it will be in the power of that Canal to draw down your water so as to injure your Navigation most materially.
>
> The depth of water in the Kennet & Avon Canal is meant to be six feet and the water in your Canal is to be four-and-a-half feet (and only four feet upon the Lock Sills) so that it will be in their power to draw off two feet and still leave moderate Navigable depth in their Canal but it would reduce nearly three miles in length of your Canal to two feet upon the Sills which would amount to almost a full stop upon the Navigation upon your Canal if not prevented by a regulating Lock such as described in the Plan annexed, to which I beg to refer.

William was also a shrewd businessman. Taking advantage of the prevailing tax laws, he had his brick kilns produce oversize bricks, which not only meant fewer bricks per lock were needed but also considerably reduced the company's tax liability. Whitworth again:

> I would recommend [them] to be made in such moulds that they will stand ten inches long, four inches and three quarters broad and three inches thick, this will require moulds ten-inches-and-a-half long, five inches wide and three-inches-and-one-sixth thick. Seven hundred of these Bricks will do as much Work as a thousand of the Common-sized Statute Bricks. The expense of making them is less in proportion to their size and more than one fourth part of the duty will be saved.

The canal progressed, and soon boats were moving along its waters. As each section was finished, one brick kiln was closed and another built nearer to the next construction site, thereby reducing the time taken to bring building materials to the workforce.

By 1810 the canal reached Abingdon, and with great celebrations the first boat completed its through voyage. As reported in the *Morning Chronicle* (19 September 1810):

The opening of the Wilts & Berks Canal into the River Thames, at Abingdon, was celebrated there on Friday last, with every demonstration of joy. At half-past-two o'clock, a body of the Proprietors, in the Company's boat, with music playing and flags flying, passed the last lock, into the River Thames, amidst the loud huzzas of a large concourse of people, who lined the sides of the Canal. The party proceeded from the banks of the Thames to the Council Chamber, where they were joined by the Members of Parliament for Cricklade, Abingdon, Oxford, Hereford, Ludgershall &c. &c. and many Gentlemen of the neighbourhood, and partook of an excellent dinner prepared for the occasion. Wm. Hallet, Esq. the Chairman, prefaced his toast of 'Success to the Wilts & Berks Canal', with a concise speech, in which he stated that the concern was in such high credit that every Proprietor who regularly proceeded on his original subscription could, at the present price of shares, obtain a cent per cent upon his capital (an advantage, at so early a period, unprecedented in the history of canals), and commented with great ability on the future prospects of the undertaking. His address was received with every mark of satisfaction, and the Proprietors, in bursts of applause, expressed how sensibly they felt their obligations to him for his many years persevering exertions as Chairman of the Committee of Management, and unanimously resolved that their thanks for his services should be presented to him, engraven on a plate of the value of 100 guineas. The day was spent with great conviviality and harmony, enlivened by many appropriate toasts and songs, until the company, highly gratified, separated at a late hour.

At the same time the Kennet & Avon Canal opened, and thus two rival undertakings began a competition for the London to Bristol trade. Who would win? Well, history shows it was the Kennet & Avon. Although more heavily locked (especially at Caen Hill!), it was a shorter route and a broader canal. It also had a joker to play. Wilts & Berks traffic had to travel over the nine miles of the Kennet & Avon between the Somersetshire Coal Canal and Semington Junction. The Kennet & Avon would charge tolls for all goods carried.

Back in the 1780s, even whilst plans for the Wilts & Berks Canal were still being formulated, there was talk of a canal (or branch) from the Thames & Severn Canal which would bypass the very difficult Upper Thames Navigation. For many reasons, including opposition from the Thames Commissioners and towns along the upper reaches of the Thames, nothing happened. The problems of navigating the tortuous route down from Lechlade to Abingdon continued until eventually it was decided that a new canal would have to be built linking the Thames & Severn to the Wilts & Berks. The route that was finally decided upon ran from Latton to Swindon, and this was opened in 1819. Imaginatively, it was called the North Wilts Canal. Within a year this canal was incorporated into the Wilts & Berks, thus becoming its North Wilts branch.

The Wilts & Berks traded modestly for a few years, paying small dividends until the Great Western Railway arrived. Then for several years business boomed as the canal carried the building materials for the benefit of the iron horse. The canal proprietors did not at first take railway competition seriously. However, they soon realised their mistake.

As the rail network expanded, so trade on the canal system declined, until, on 31 August 1874, the *Swindon Advertiser* reported:

A meeting of the Shareholders in this company was held at the Queen's Hotel, New Swindon, on Friday morning last, for the purpose of considering a proposition made by certain of the shareholders to apply to Parliament for permission to close or sell the canal, the property of the shareholders. The chair was taken by Major Power, Chairman of the Company, and there were twenty-two shareholders present.

The meeting lasted two hours, and, after much discussion, the proposition was defeated.

What to do? Improve the canal, reduce tolls or look for new business? All this was tried by several different owners, but still the trade slowly disappeared.

In the early 1880s a new consortium leased the concern, determined to restore the waterway and regenerate the trade upon it. They attempted to use 'Sectional Boats', which were built with 'approved stem and stern, and body like a centipede, the individual sections, about the length of a railway truck, could be detached and be left at the wharves en route.' Unfortunately, this new design could neither be steered nor properly loaded, the body separated at inconvenient times, and the whole vessel was found unsuitable for navigating the River Avon. The scheme failed and the old boats continued to be used for the traffic. The proprietors worked the canal at a loss, and eventually, on payment of a large sum, they were released from their obligations and the canal reverted to the previous owner.

Even the involvement of Lord Wantage failed to help the ailing navigation, and finally in a fit of pique the canal blew an artery and bled to death. Or, to be clinically accurate, in 1901 a large section of one of the arches of the Stanley Aqueduct on the main line between Chippenham and Calne collapsed and the canal simply drained into the River Marden. (Conspiracy theorists might think this was rather convenient, given the recent failed attempts to abandon the canal.) This effectively stopped all through trade on the canal, although some boat movements carried on for a while on either side of the break. The canal owners seized the opportunity to try once again to abandon the canal. But this proved no easy matter and it would take many years to accomplish. In Swindon, the state of the degenerating waterway caused a great deal of worry. A medical health report in June 1908 raised serious concerns about the state of the canal, as the following extract illustrates:

> From Graham Street to Skurray's Mill and Whale Bridge, there is less water. Opposite the brick kilns there is a surface collection of stinking filth, and from here to the mill and bridge the water is black and stinking. From Whale Bridge to Wellington Street the canal is overgrown, but the smell of the water is offensive. From Wellington Street Bridge to the junction and on the Regent Street Bridge the water is clear of weed and is black and very offensive.

Unfortunately for the proprietors of the canal, it was 1914 before the canal could be legally abandoned, by which time Swindon and the other towns were only too keen to get rid of the 'stinking ditch'. So the Wilts & Berks Canal passed into history.

The Kennet & Avon Canal was more fortunate, having been purchased by the Great Western Railway (GWR), and it continued to be used until the 1960s when 'the authorities' finally attempted to close it. The long battle that followed to save and re-establish this fine waterway is well-documented.

When the Wilts & Berks Canal was abandoned, its assets were disposed of. Land was either sold or returned to its original owners. Responsibility for the canal and the various road bridges in the towns passed to the relevant authorities. Provision was also made for the protection of water supplies to farms and local businesses. It was in the towns that the closure of the canal became a problem. With very little movement of the water, the canal soon became overgrown with weed, silted up and eventually stagnated. The canal bed also provided a very convenient place for the dumping of rubbish. Fears were raised over the effect this was having on the health of the local populace. But it would be many years before the canal was finally obliterated from these towns. In the countryside, through which most of the canal ran, the line only very slowly deteriorated. Some sections were filled in and ploughed over and other parts were built on, but most of it was surrendered to Mother Nature. Over the years many bridges and locks were destroyed, and in several cases the bricks pilfered for other building projects. On his return from India in 1919, Alfred Williams, the well-respected Swindon author, recalls how he and Mary, his wife, spent many weeks gathering building materials from a 'tumble-down lock', the hard physical work exhausting them. By 1921 they had built a substantial home which they called by the Indian name 'Ranikhet', which still exists. The materials almost certainly came from the South Marston locks. It is also recorded that bricks from the Dunnington locks were used to build houses in Wootton Bassett.

A major act of vandalism occurred in the 1960s when, in order to allow easy access for construction lorries running back and forth from Didcot Power Station, many of the remaining arch bridges in the area were demolished. Other bridges were destroyed as part of road improvement schemes and urban developments. The few bridges that did escape destruction – and these were mainly farm accommodation bridges – still suffered from local vandalism and the general effects of a lack of maintenance. By the 1980s, only the Shrivenham Road Bridge was still performing its original function, although the canal over which it passed was stagnant and filled with rubbish. Strangely enough, the Stanley Aqueduct remained standing, albeit with a big hole in it, and did not collapse until the 1990s.

For many years small communities continued to exist along the canal line in places almost unknown to the general population. At Latton Junction, Alfred and Anne Howse were, with their children, the residents of the Toll House. In the 1881 census Anne is shown as the toll collector and Alfred as a general labourer. When the canal was abandoned, Alfred bought the cottage, after the Earl of St Germans had declined to purchase it, and continued to live there until his death in 1937. The cottage stayed in family hands until the 1950s and still exists today. The remote Ardington Mead Farm was by the canal close to Ardington Top Lock, near Grove, and on the opposite bank to it was a bungalow. Known as 'Canalside Cottages', the buildings were inhabited until the 1960s by the Potter family, with 'Uncle Jim' living in the bungalow. There was also a lock-keeper's cottage, but this was uninhabited. The farm and the bungalow were demolished shortly after the family left. Chaddington lock-keeper Alfred Woodward and his wife Elizabeth continued to live in the lock cottage with their family. Charles Hunt was the last lock-keeper at Seven Locks. He purchased the land and buildings at the top of the locks and lived there for many years. There are many other examples of individuals and families living on in buildings previously owned by the canal company or used for canal business.

As the years passed, the inevitable destruction continued as urban development/rural encroachment continued. But, against the odds, much of the canal lingered on until late in the 1970s when its 'discovery' led to the active restoration that is now taking place. All along the line of the old canal structures are being re-built, country sections returned to water and plans formulated to overcome the more complicated problems such as the M4 crossing, and possibly restoring the route through Swindon. A new junction with the River Thames has been opened just a mile downstream from the original in Abingdon and new junctions have been identified at Semington on the Kennet & Avon Canal and at Eisey (replacing Latton) on the Thames & Severn Canal, both necessary as the old canal line in these places is no longer currently viable.

Following the successful re-opening of the Kennet & Avon Canal, and because it is certain that the Stroudwater and Thames & Severn Canals will be restored for navigation in the foreseeable future, it is just a matter of time, money and foresight before the Wilts & Berks Canal assumes its rightful place at the centre of a Wessex Waterways Network.

Note: When describing the pictures in this book I have assumed the canal Main Line to run east to west and the North Wilts branch to run north to south. This is not strictly accurate because, as with all canals, the Wilts & Berks twists and turns. This is just to simplify the descriptions.

1

ABINGDON TO
ARDINGTON

Horse-drawn narrowboats waiting at the entrance of the junction in Abingdon in the early 1800s. On the other side of the bridge was the lock which had a rise of 9ft 6in and led directly into the basin.

This watercolour, by local artist William Waite, shows the original stone bridge over the River Ock, with the Old Anchor Inn and St Helens church in the background. The stone bridge was replaced by the canal company with a cast-iron bridge, which is still in place and, apart from being widened in August 1991, remains unchanged.

An excellent drawing of the junction bridge with the balance arm of the bottom gate shown in fine detail by an unknown early nineteenth-century artist.

The canal bridge can be seen just to the left of the warehouse. On the other side of the junction stands the iron works, then the River Ock Bridge, the Old Anchor and St Helens church, *c*.1900.

The narrowboat moored at St Helens Wharf (around 1905) had probably not come off the canal, as trade on the canal after 1900 was practically nonexistent. Other means of earning a living needed to be found. Hiring out skiffs on the river was very popular.

The landlady of the Old Anchor Inn, a popular stopover for boatmen for very many years, was able to supplement her income by using the wharf. Her daughter Ruby, who worked on the skiffs and still lives nearby, recalls that her mother insisted on making her a pair of trousers to maintain her dignity whilst leaping over the boats. This picture was taken around 1920.

This old iron boat was salvaged from its shallow resting place at the Abingdon School boathouse at the end of Wilsham Road, Abingdon, in the summer of 1992. It is assumed to have been built in the boatyard at the Abingdon Junction, which specialised in iron boats. Although it is thought to have been used on the canal, its purpose is unknown.

Although Jack Dalby described the Wilts & Berks as a 'mean little canal', the company certainly did not skimp on some of the managers' buildings, as seen here in Abingdon, c.1960. This very substantial house, which still stands today, was obviously meant to impress potential users and investors.

By the 1960s Junction Bridge and the lock had disappeared, although the warehouse still remains today. The Nissan-type hut is built directly over the lock.

Looking back at the river from where the top gates of the lock would have been, c.1970. The hut has now been removed. Local residents state that the lock is still basically intact under the concrete and that this was confirmed a few years ago when some building excavations were made.

An aerial shot of the river shows the junction on the bend with the site of the basin and the canal line still well defined, c.1960.

Looking back along the towpath, alongside Caldecott Road, the bridge is raised but there is no sign of activity, c.1900. It is difficult to believe that there are no known pictures of the canal and basin with working boats.

The lift bridge at the far end of the basin is shown in this nineteenth-century drawing. All the area is now buried under modern housing developments and there is no possibility of the canal ever being reinstated along the historic route through Abingdon.

Looking from the Basin along the dry bed of the canal alongside Caldecott Road in the 1920s.

2006 was an historic year in the history of the canal. It was in this year that it was officially reconnected to the waterways system; and a new junction, about one mile downstream from the original in Abingdon, was constructed opposite Culham Cut on the River Thames. The work was carried out by contractors as well as local volunteers and members of Waterway Recovery Group, and was partially funded by a grant from the Inland Waterways Association. Although not very long, this new section of canal will eventually be extended to rejoin the original line.

The new junction was officially opened in August 2006. The ceremony was attended by local dignitaries and representatives of all supporting organisations. The first boat to enter the canal was the Inland Waterways Association boat *Jubilee*, followed by a host of other vessels, many of which were returning from the IWA National Festival held at Beale Park.

All along the canal during its working life, small basins and wharves grew as local requirements dictated. Henry de Salis' boat *Dragon Fly* is moored in Steventon Basin. In the distance is Cow Common Bridge, 1895.

Cow Common Bridge on the Hanney Road in the 1950s. This was a bridge without a towpath and must have been frustrating for the skippers of the horse-drawn boats. It was soon to disappear under road improvement schemes.

Above: Two miles north-east of Wantage lay a small settlement by the canal which, by its very remoteness, managed to remain almost intact from 1914 until the mid-1960s. It consisted of Ardingtonmead Farm and a small bungalow. They are now long gone, although demolition rubble is still evident when the field is ploughed. The distant embankment carried the main GWR line. This image is from around 1950.

Left: Mr and Mrs Potter went to live at the farm in the 1930s with their daughter Dolly and sons Clifford and Ernie. A bungalow on the opposite side of the canal was inhabited by 'Uncle Jim', who worked for Ardington Wick Farm. These ladies are Dolly (Rivers) and her mother. The building behind is the outdoor 'privy', *c.*1954.

Left: Mr Potter with an ancient petrol mower, keeping the towpath clear, *c.*1954. The canal is immediately to the left.

Below: 'Uncle Jim's' bungalow lacked, as did the farm, all modern amenities. He would even have had to cross the canal to get fresh water from the only tap in the farm. No trace remains of the building today, although it was still there in 1963.

2

AROUND
WANTAGE

The road that passes over Pinmarsh Bridge was originally a private drive constructed by Colonel Robert Lloyd-Lindsay, Lord Wantage, in the nineteenth century. This afforded him, his family and guests a faster and more convenient route between Wantage Road Station, which has long been closed, and Lockinge House, where he lived. This photograph was taken around 1890.

Grove Common Lock is the third lock down the Grove flight of six. In the 1920s it still contained water, although at a low level, and apparently fish as well. The tail-bridge was rebuilt by volunteers in the 1990s, but as yet the future of the lock has not been decided upon.

Seen in 1947 just west of Grove Bridge, this bungalow stands alongside the dried bed of the canal. Currently this line is still intact through Lime Kiln Lock as far as Grove Top Lock. The section between Lime Kiln and Grove Top Lock was dredged and re-watered in the 1990s.

The bungalow shown in the previous picture is in the top right of this aerial view, just west of Grove Bridge, c.1946. The line can be seen heading west through Lime Kiln Lock to Grove Top Lock, which is just before the filled-in junction with the Wantage arm. The canal at the end of the runway has been filled in, obviously for the safety of overshooting aircraft.

A few hundred yards west of Grove Bridge the canal was carried over the Letcombe Brook on a stone aqueduct, pictured here in 1964. The bungalow shown in the previous picture is in the top left corner.

An unidentified lock on the Grove Flight, c.1890.

Looking east at Grove Top Lock, c.1890. The tail-bridge can be seen, and to the left is the lock-keeper's cottage. Just behind the photographer is the junction with the Wantage arm.

A rare sight: a narrowboat at the junction facing Grove Top Lock, possibly waiting to pass through, c.1895. It is probable that the boat has come from Wantage Wharf.

Belmont Bridge on the Wantage arm was still in excellent condition when this photograph was taken, looking towards the town. The date is unknown.

The scene at Wantage Wharf in the 1890s. The wharf still looks fairly busy and is in good, clean condition. The boat would have been horse-drawn, seeing as no mechanically powered trading boat ever operated on the canal.

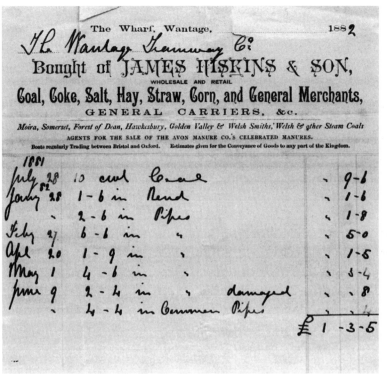

The Wharf, Wantage.   1882

The Wantage Tramway Co.

Bought of JAMES HISKINS & SON,

WHOLESALE AND RETAIL

Coal, Coke, Salt, Hay, Straw, Corn, and General Merchants,

GENERAL CARRIERS, &c.

Moira, Somerset, Forest of Dean, Hawkesbury, Golden Valley & Welsh Smiths,' Welsh & other Steam Coals

AGENTS FOR THE SALE OF THE AVON MANURE CO.'S CELEBRATED MANURES.

Boats regularly Trading between Bristol and Oxford.   Estimates given for the Conveyance of Goods to any part of the Kingdom.

1881

July 28	10 cwt Coal		"	9-6
Jany 28	1-6 in Bend		"	1-6
"	2-6 in Pipes		"	1-8
Feby 27	6-1 in "		"	5-0
Apl 20	1-9 in "		"	1-5
May 1	4-6 in "		"	3-4
June 9	2-4 in " damaged		"	.8
"	4-4 in Common Pipes		"	.4

£ 1 -3-5

The wharf was for many years very prosperous and, as shown on this invoice from 1881-82, even brought in goods for the Wantage Tramway.

Although there are two narrowboats tied up at the wharf, by the end of the nineteenth century trade was diminishing and weeds had started to encroach into the basin.

A few years later, the boats have gone and the weeds have almost completely taken over. The wharf crane was eventually sold to the Wantage Tramway and used in their maintenance yard. Where it went after that is not known.

Wantage church looms over the sad looking wharf, which is almost unrecognisable. Although the canal branch into the town was still there in the 1960s, it was just an overgrown ditch.

The wharf buildings survived for many years and the land was used for various purposes including a lorry repair business, as this picture of a large 'pit' in 1960 shows.

The wharfinger's house in 1960. The whole of the wharf and basin area has now been redeveloped as a housing estate. All the old buildings, except for this one and the Sack House, have now gone.

Sack House in 1960, still in existence thanks to local campaigners who had to fight to prevent it from being demolished.

Back on the main line of the canal looking east towards Hunters Bridge, *c.*1900. This stretch of the canal was cleared and re-watered by volunteers in the 1990s.

There are many stories of people ice-skating on the canal during the hard Victorian winters. Journeys from Wantage to Abingdon are recorded. These skaters are on the eastern side of Hunters Bridge, *c*.1890.

Looking west at the skaters by Kings Lift Bridge, near East Challow, *c*.1890. Although the remains of the lift bridge were replaced with a fixed platform in 1979, plans are being drawn for its reinstatement as a lift bridge.

In 2005 the East Vale (Wantage) branch of the Wilts & Berks Canal Trust rebuilt a long section of a stone wharf near Childrey. Originally the wharf was used to transport bricks from the local Kiln. In the future it will provide a very pleasant overnight mooring for pleasure boats.

A team photo at the rebuilt wharf. This group is typical of the many teams working along the canal line, restoring and rebuilding the old canal with the ultimate aim of returning the waterway to full use for the benefit of the local communities.

3

UFFINGTON TO JOHN STREET JUNCTION

The GWR main line crossing the filled-in canal bridge (looking east from near Longcot), *c*.1960.

One of the Longcot locks, *c*.1890.

Looking west at the GWR viaduct crossing the canal at Acorn Bridge in the 1950s. The canal arch is now part of the A420.

Although the canal under the viaduct appears to be filled in, the towpath looks fairly well used.

South Marston Top Lock in the late 1890s. The man with the 'dolly' is probably Shadrach, the blind son of John Ferris the lock-keeper.

South Marston Top Lock Cottage in the 1960s. This was originally two cottages, but they were converted into a single residence some time after the canal closed.

Looking east at Stratton Wharf in the late 1800s. It is now long gone under an ever-expanding Swindon.

Marsh Farm stone arch bridge, *c*.1960. The bridge still exists just east of Swindon's 'Magic Roundabout', although a footpath now passes under the arch.

Looking east at the stone arch of Drove Road Bridge in 1880. It was demolished in 1922. This is now the site of the 'Magic Roundabout'.

Looking east from what is now the site of the 'Magic Roundabout' in the late 1950s. The canal is to the right of the garage.

The canal manager's house, Fairholme, was looking very dilapidated in the 1940s and had very little resemblance to William Cobbett's description in his *Rural Rides*.

By the 1940s Dunsford's Wharf had been turned into a council depot.

Popular Swindon photographer William Hooper took this picture of his sister-in-law Alice Richards with her sons Stanley and Leslie, *c*.1905. They are looking west towards York Road Bridge, and Dunsford's Wharf can be seen in the background.

Striding out east from York Road Bridge, this gentleman is more interested in the photographer than in the empty narrowboat on the opposite bank, *c*.1900.

York Road Bridge was demolished to make way for the construction of Fleming Way, June 1961.

The abutments of York Road Bridge still stand today, but the northern one was moved to allow for the added width of the new road, June 1961.

Whale Bridge in the 1950s. The canal runs west from the right-hand side of the picture. The small structure on the bridge is a gents' toilet.

Looking west from Whale Bridge with the Whale Hotel on the left and Skurrays Mill down the canal on the right, October 1959.

Looking back at Whale Bridge along the canal bed which has been in-filled with drainage pipes being laid along it, June 1960.

In the late 1800s mill owner Mr Skurray became one of the first people in the Swindon area to own a motor vehicle. Working in his mill was an employee who possessed an aptitude for repairing motor cars, and Mr Skurray, seeing a business opportunity, founded Skurrays Motor Garage in 1899. In 1926 they teamed up with General Motors and were the first garage in the country to place a bulk order for Vauxhall cars.

On 21 March 1958, record player manufacturer Garrards factory, situated close to the canal line, was hit by Swindon's worst fire ever. Skurray's Mill is to the left of the picture.

Wellington Street Bridge, c.1890. Just east of the junction with the North Wilts branch, this was sometimes known as Queenstown Bridge.

4

NORTH WILTS
BRANCH

John Street Junction, *c.*1922. The main line of the canal runs left to right and the North Wilts branch heads down towards the GWR station.

Looking south at John Street Bridge, *c.*1900. It was a stone arch bridge that was demolished early in the 1920s.

The unique iron trellis Bullens Bridge shortly before its demolition in the early 1920s.

Not one thing or another, the canal passed under the railway by way of numerous bridges which were added as the GWR grew, and these effectively became a tunnel. The line of the canal follows the footpath across the rails, c.1900.

Left: When the original lock-keeper left Swindon Top Lock, the Pope family moved in and lived there for many years. There were eleven children, three boys and eight girls. These are four of the daughters, Iris, Edith, Muriel and Nora, posing by the top of the lock, *c.*1930.

Below: Although it had only very basic facilities, the cottage was inhabited until the 1930s. Fresh water had to be carried from a water point some 200 yards away across the recreational ground. This photograph was taken around 1920.

Moredon Power Station was built over the canal line and the canal bed was used as a dump for the station's waste products. The canal runs from the bottom left, and in the centre Moredon Lock Cottage can be seen, *c.*1945.

There were many water mills along the proposed canal route, and in order to prevent disputes over water, the Canal Company would attempt to purchase them. Newman's Mill on the River Ray escaped this fate.

In the late 1990s Purton Road was upgraded. Incorporated into the scheme was a navigable culvert for the canal and a footpath.

The remains of Pry Lock in June 1962. Pry Farm can be seen in the distance.

Pry Farm at the end of the nineteenth century. The taller of the two figures is Mrs Mary Ody. The farm is still in use today.

Crosslanes Lock with tail-bridge, c.1956. The name is derived from the adjacent crossroads, and the remains of the lock are now buried in the cottage garden.

Well into the 1960s sections of the North Wilts remained in remarkably untouched condition. This is the view towards the north from the Newth's Lane crossing, September 1961.

The aqueduct over the River Key was threatened with demolition as its poor state was preventing the efficient run-off of flood water. Volunteers quickly took action and now, with the aid of National Lottery money, the structure has been completely renovated.

Chelworth Wharf was situated just before the southern portal of Cricklade Tunnel. As with many of the canal properties, it remained relatively unchanged for many years. The canal ran past the right-hand side of the building. This picture was taken in September 1961.

Entrance to Chelworth Wharf, September 1961. The line of the canal was behind the buildings.

The dry canal bed at Cricklade leading up to one of the three Wilts & Berks tunnels, *c*.1960. Sadly, urban development led to the in-filling of the tunnel and effectively blocked the use of this line for a restored canal. The Wilts & Berks Canal Trust have an alternative plan to route the canal east of the town to a new junction with the Thames & Severn Canal at Eisey.

The River Thames is flowing fast under the canal aqueduct in 1897. This has now been replaced by a footbridge, but a similar aqueduct still exists at Latton Basin.

The regulating lock at Latton Basin, 1890. The lock prevented water from the Swindon summit being drained away into the Thames & Severn Canal. The haystacks are in fact thatched sheds.

Latton Basin as seen from the bottom gates of the lock. The bridge is at the junction with the Thames & Severn Canal. By the 1930s the weeds had started to take over.

The basin actually belonged to the Thames & Severn Canal and was joined to it by a short aqueduct over the Churn Mill Leat. The aqueduct was probably removed in the 1950s and the entrance to the basin was blocked off.

By 1960 the owners of the cottage had found a new use for the basin – a pig-pen.

The junction bridge seen from the edge of the basin, looking across the Mill Leat, with the aqueduct still intact, *c*.1930. The Thames & Severn Canal is on the other side of the bridge.

This is the junction bridge as seen from the far side of the Thames & Severn Canal, *c*.1930. When the bridge was destroyed, the abutments were left in place and are currently being excavated by volunteers.

When the canal was finally abandoned in 1914, Basin Cottage was purchased by Alfred Howse, who had been lock-keeper since the early 1880s when he moved in with Ann, his new bride. Members of the Howse family continued to live there until about 1950.

Although it was a very small cottage with no facilities, Ann and Alfred raised eleven children: three boys and eight daughters. One son died at an early age and another died, after serving in the First World War, from influenza. All the others lived to a ripe old age, the girls into their nineties, and one, Prudence, lived to be 100. The proud parents are seen here with their daughters and two sons, c.1900.

5

JOHN STREET JUNCTION
TO WESTLEAZE

John Street Junction with the North Wilts branch to the right and looking west at Golden Lion Bridge, *c.*1890.

The ornate and unique Golden Lion Bridge on the Wilts & Berks Canal, *c.*1900. This bridge was demolished in 1918.

*c.*1900. Golden Lion Bridge got its name from the adjacent public house, which had a large stone lion on its roof. It was noticed that whenever a tram passed by the pub the lion wobbled. For safety reasons it was taken down and placed in a fenced-off area outside the pub.

The lion was eventually put into council storage, and during the big freeze of winter 1963 a tarpaulin was placed over it for protection. Unfortunately, the humid conditions caused the stone to crumble beyond repair. The children seen here in the 1950s are Christopher Pike (in the pram) with his brother David and his sister Victoria. To mark the Queen's Silver Jubilee, on 25 February 1978, a modern replica was erected in Swindon's Canal Walk.

One of Swindon's new trams approaching Golden Lion Bridge, c.1905. Although the canal was not yet officially abandoned, all boat traffic had effectively ceased. It is doubtful that the bridge could still be raised as the tram lines appear to be continuous over it.

The corporation started to operate the electric trams in 1904. In 1906 the 'Swindon Tram Disaster' occurred. A No.11 tram taking passengers from the Bath & West Show being held in the old town suffered brake failure driving down Victoria Hill and crashed, killing several people and injuring many more.

Looking west from the site of Golden Lion Bridge in June 1961.

This sign survived for many years along the filled-in old canal. Swindon Council is currently leading the project to reinstate the canal line through the town. No doubt the new signs will indicate that it is a cycle-way.

Milton Road Bridge, shown here in around 1970, still stands. The overhanging section of the Central Club apparently had no connection with the canal running below.

Cambria Bridge, seen here around 1960, still exists, although modifications were carried out in 1978.

Swindon did not completely ignore the old canal. Artist Ken White painted fine murals on either side of Cambria Bridge in 1982.

This is the other side! Unfortunately the murals have not survived.

Webb's Warehouse and Wharf, *c.*1880. Cambria Bridge is just out of the picture on the left.

Looking east towards Marlborough Street Bridge, *c.*1914. This was a steel footbridge and it was demolished in the 1920s, by which time the canal would have been in-filled.

The stone arch Kingshill Bridge looking west, *c*.1900. It was also known for a time as Rushey Platt Bridge, although, confusingly, this was also the name given to a wooden drawbridge further west that was demolished in 1883.

Looking back at Kingshill Bridge. The bridge was demolished around 1921. If the plan to take the canal back through Swindon goes ahead then the canal line will have to pass under this road again – an interesting engineering problem, as there is no headroom under the existing road.

The arrival in 1881 of the Midland & South Western Junction Railway necessitated a large embankment and a substantial bridge over the canal. Seen here shortly after it was built, the bridge is now known locally as Skew Bridge.

At Westleaze the canal has been restored and will once again become part of the route through Swindon if the current plans are implemented. Looking east, with Skew Bridge in the centre, 2005.

Beavans Bridge, *c.*1900, from the west side, was probably demolished in the 1930s. A replica was built in 2000 by Wilts & Berks Canal Trust volunteers.

Rebuilding Beavens Bridge generated a lot of local interest. Chief bricklayer Ron Robertson is seen here doing his Pied Piper impression, leading children from Lethbridge Junior School over the bridge in May 2000.

Restored and re-watered sections of canal need constant attention. Swindon volunteers use a custom-made weed-cutting boat to keep the water clear.

A new housing estate is planned for the area adjacent to the canal at Westleaze. In preparation for the influx of new residents several new bridges have had to be built over the River Ray and this one over the canal. This is a 2009 view.

6

AROUND
WOOTTON BASSETT

Wroughton Wharf, *c.*1925. Although the canal will never come back this way the building is still in use by the farm.

Looking back at Wroughton Wharf from Elcombe Bridge, *c.*1960.

This painting from 1916 shows Elcombe Farm Bridge between Wroughton and Hay Lane wharves.

Mr and Mrs Frank Little lived at Hay Lane Wharf from the early 1900s until 1964. Although Frank worked for the GWR, he also had a smallholding at the wharf. His granddaughter remembers swinging out over the canal and in the winter ice-skating on it. This picture was taken in August 1962.

Looking west at a dry canal bed from Binknoll Road Bridge towards Chaddington Top (Summit) Lock, *c*.1960.

The bridge was not to last much longer and, like so many, it was culverted and demolished.

Over four decades later and the canal below Binknoll Road Bridge has been excavated and profiled as far as Chaddington Top Lock. Both sides of the bridge have been cleared and plans to rebuild it are now well advanced.

With the rapid expansion of Swindon comes the problem of surface water run-off from the town. It is expected that the restored canal will be used to carry much of this away. In anticipation of this, a large new spill weir has been built by volunteers just below Binknoll Road Bridge.

Left: Alfred Woodward was the last lock-keeper at Chaddington. Seen here in around 1890 with his wife Elizabeth (*née* Grimshaw) who, like so many young girls of the time, was 'in service' before getting married.

Below: In Victorian times very large families were common. Hard as a lock-keeper's life was, it must have been healthy for here are Alfred and Elizabeth with their five daughters and five sons, *c.*1916.

By this time (August 1962) the thousands of bricks used in the construction of the lock had disappeared, probably to some local building project. The canal bed down to the lower Chaddington Lock was dry.

June 1978. Chaddington Lock Cottage has either been demolished or simply just collapsed.

The lock cottage may have gone, but Chaddington Top Lock has been completely rebuilt by volunteers with the addition of a tail-bridge for farm access. The official opening of the bridge took place on 13 April 2005.

The re-watered one mile Templars Firs section has been the site of several boat rallies, and the honour of being the first narrowboat on the cut goes to *The Harry Hunt* in 1996.

The Bridge Inn (September 1959) was situated alongside the canal. It survived into the 1960s when it was converted into a private residence.

This is probably how Wootton Bassett Town Hall would have looked in the 1790s when the initial meetings of the canal proposers took place. The Crimean War cannon, however, would not have been there at that time.

Looking east towards Marlborough Road from the site of Dunnington Top Lock in September 1962. Although the canal is now filled in, the line is still clear.

As with the other locks in this area, the bricks have gone, although the gate posts still stand. Dunnington Lock Cottage is in the background. This picture was taken in September 1962.

Dunnington Lock Cottage still standing and possibly inhabited in September 1962, as indicated by the TV aerial. It has since been demolished.

Trickles Lane Bridge suffered the same fate as most of the other bridges, being culverted and demolished. Dunnington Lock Cottage is in the background, *c*.1960.

Peter Smith, restoration director for the Wilts & Berks Canal Amenity Group (now WBCT) at the time, is inspecting Dunnington Top Lock which was cleared in the 1990s. As both the Dunnington locks are in the countryside they will be relatively simple to rebuild.

Dunnington aqueduct was an early restoration site. In 2008 the local Wootton Bassett branch of WBCT returned to the site. They have cleared the scrub from around the arches and will soon be turning their attention to the canal bed.

7

SEVEN LOCKS,
DAUNTSEY AND FOXHAM

West of Vastern Wharf is the isolated Hart Farm accommodation bridge, c.1960. The current condition of the bridge is unknown.

These young ladies are posing on Trow Lane Bridge, c.1930. Elsie Lewis is in the white dress. The canal is obviously already overgrown at this time, but the line today is still viable.

Left: Charles Hunt, the last lock-keeper on the Seven Locks flight, *c.*1910. He was born in 1862 and died at the age of eighty-one in 1943. After its abandonment, Charles bought the land and buildings at the top of the locks and continued to live there.

Below: The stables are on the left, the canal going east, and Charles is with his donkey, *c.*1910.

Fifty years later and the scene at the top of Seven Locks has not changed a great deal. The dried bed of the canal is still very obvious, *c.*1960.

Early in the 1970s the stables are still in good condition. The top lock of Seven Locks is just to the left, out of the picture. Unfortunately access to the area, which includes locks six and seven, is not currently permitted.

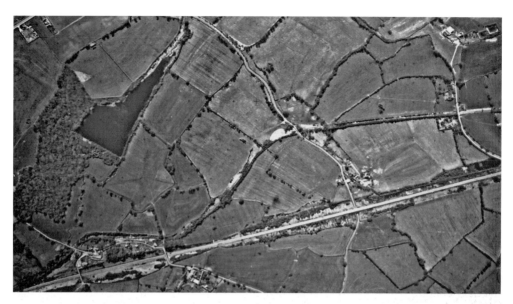

Tockenham Reservoir fed the canal using a feeder above Seven Locks. Left to right, the canal runs down through the flight of locks, across Bowds Lane towards Waite Hill Farm, with the GWR main line running in a much straighter line in the same direction, c.1950.

In spite of the access restrictions at the top of the Seven Locks flight, work continues on the lower locks. Lock three has been totally reconstructed and lock four (inset) is nearly finished. Preparatory work on locks one and two has been done and plans to rebuild the Bowds Lane Bridge are being prepared. All the work is being carried out by volunteers. These photographs were taken in 2008.

Hidden under all this scrub, in May 1965, is Dauntsey Lock. There is an interesting collection of vehicles in the pub car park which are possibly something to do with Barnes' Garage, which is on the opposite side of the road.

Closer inspection reveals the remains of the bottom gates still in position, May 1965.

This view from Clack Hill has the canal running across the picture with the Peterborough Arms, Hope House and the Dauntsey Wharf buildings clearly shown, *c*.1905.

Although not directly related to the canal, these two fine steam rollers, pausing for the photographer on their long journey up the hill from Dauntsey Lock, are some indication of the modern technology that was making the horse-drawn narrowboat obsolete, *c*.1905.

The Peterborough Arms was originally a farm house, as seen here, *c*.1890. The canal buildings and lock are to the left of the picture.

By the start of the First World War the farm house had already been turned into a public house, and it remains so today. In the not-too-distant future it is hoped that boats will again be using the pub wharf.

By the 1970s the canal buildings at Dauntsey Lock were derelict. The lock in the foreground has been filled with some sort of building material, presumably dumped on top of the bottom gates.

The buildings by Dauntsey Wharf were in much the same state. All have now been renovated.

The rise in the road just beyond the buildings is the site of the Dauntsey Lock tail-bridge, looking towards Clack Hill, *c*.1960. On the right is Hope House which, during the 1800s, was a public house known as the The Lamb. Barnes' Garage is facing The Peterborough Arms.

The rear entrance to Dauntsey Wharf, *c*.1960. The small building on the right is the weighbridge, which still exists today.

Volunteers have constructed this farm access lift bridge just above Foxham Top Lock, and an enterprising local resident has built his own boat. This photograph was taken in 2005.

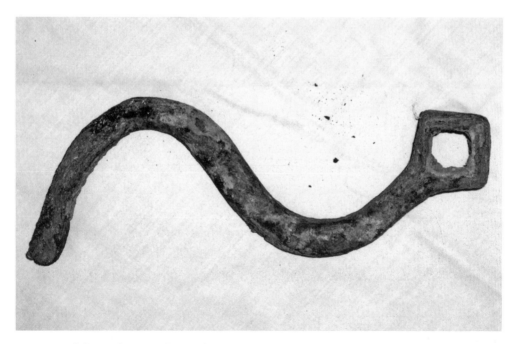

In 1988, whilst working on the top lock at Foxham, John Harrod discovered this very unusual windlass in the canal bed. Look at it closely and you will see that the operator would have had to use a very different technique than with a conventional windlass.

Left: Foxham Top Lock was the first lock to be rebuilt by volunteers in the 1980s. It showed just what could be achieved with limited resources but with unlimited professional enthusiasm.

Below: The tail-bridge was also rebuilt, and although the canal bed just below the lock is being used as a garden, there are no obstructions between here and the lower lock, *c.*1990.

May 1965 and the canal between the two locks was clear except for the weeds. Even today it would require only a relatively minor amount of work to reinstate it.

The remains of Foxham Bottom Lock in May 1965. As with many other locks, much of the brickwork has been re-used, but the chamber is basically sound.

Left: Foxham Bottom Lock was eventually cleared in the 1980s, preparatory to rebuilding, and the remains were found to be in a fairly stable condition.

Below: Unfortunately work was unable to proceed at that time and the landowner decided for safety reasons to back-fill the lock chamber.

8

CALNE TO
CHIPPENHAM

The Harris bacon factory dominated Calne for many years. Calne Wharf is behind the town hall (the building with the clock tower) on the right of the picture, *c*.1950.

The Harris factory overlooks the River Marden and faces Calne Wharf, *c*.1960. The water level in the river is no longer regulated for boats so it is very low.

Flooding is not a new occurrence. In the late 1950s the River Marden broke over its banks and flooded the town. Much of this water could have been carried away by the canal if it had not been abandoned and in-filled.

Marden House was home to the Wharfinger who handled traffic on the Wilts & Berks Canal, which terminated here. Local people raised funds and obtained grants to renovate the building and converted it to a community and arts centre. Prince Charles gave his support by visiting in 1988, and it was officially opened in 1990.

This aerial photograph, probably from the 1950s, clearly shows the River Marden flowing past the wharf and making a sharp turn towards the location of Town Lock. The sluice gates used for maintaining the water levels, known as 'The Hatches', can be seen at the bottom of the picture. The course of the river flows through these gates.

Seen from a different angle, the river flows out of the top of the picture. 'The Hatches' are hidden by the trees on the bend. This also shows the site of Town Lock, which appears to be covered by bushes.

Calne Wharf, *c.*1960. The River Marden flows behind the stables and past the wharfinger's house.

The stables on Calne Wharf, *c.*1960. The river is behind the photographer.

Left: The water pump stands by the bridge leading to the wharf. It is still there today.

Below: The bridge over the River Marden with the very substantial wharfinger's house behind, *c.*1960.

Looking towards the town hall at the beginning of the twentieth century.

'The Hatches' controlled the level of the water flowing down the River Marden. Town Lock is to the left and the excess water goes through the sluice gates on the right, c.1905.

The remains of the sluices could still be seen in 1965.

Looking back up the river at the remains of 'The Hatches', with the Harris factory dominating the area.

Calne Town Lock is just discernable in the lower middle section of the picture, c.1890. The River Marden runs through 'The Hatches' and out of the bottom of the picture.

Chaveywell Bridge is a short distance down the canal from the lock. In the 1970s it was in a very sorry state. Fortunately the area was selected as an early restoration site and the bridge was rebuilt by volunteers.

A little way down the Calne branch is this lift bridge at Mosses Mill, *c.*1900.

Just a bit further on is another lift bridge which can be seen behind the boy in this family group. It is the same boy who is in the previous picture, sitting on the bridge.

Black Dog Tunnel was one of only three tunnels on the Wilts & Berks Canal. It took the Calne branch of the canal under what is now the A4. This is the north portal in April 1965.

The south portal of the tunnel in April 1965. It is probable that the tunnel, although in-filled, is still in reasonable condition. Explorers today can still see the top of this portal poking through the grass.

The bed of Stanley Aqueduct, seen here in the 1970s, has this very large hole in it. Was this the section that collapsed in 1901 causing the eventual abandonment of the canal?

Although now almost totally obliterated, in the 1960s sections of the Chippenham branch of the canal were still in water. This is Deep Cutting Bridge, and it looks to be in very good condition.

A little further down the Chippenham branch there was a lift bridge known as 'England's Bridge', *c.*1890.

One of the other three canal tunnels was close to Chippenham Wharf. In the autumn of 1971 the Chippenham Borough Surveyor conducted an inspection. It was even considered safe enough to take a boat into the 100-yard tunnel – the last vessel ever to enter it.

Chippenham Wharf is behind the buildings in the centre of the picture, *c.*1900.

A final view of Chippenham Wharf. Its remains were briefly exposed during redevelopment of the area in 2006.

9

PEWSHAM TO SEMINGTON

Just beyond the junction with the Chippenham branch are the three Pewsham locks. The short flight is now being restored by volunteers. This is the tail-bridge of the top lock in 2008.

Alongside the middle lock are the remains of a dry dock. Boats entered from the pound above and water was let out by means of a sluice gate set into the structure.

Double Bridge, near Reybridge, has been rebuilt by volunteers. The unusual width of the bridge is the subject for much speculation as no documentary evidence is available to support any theory.

In May 2009 HRH the Duchess of Cornwall, who is Patron of the Wilts & Berks Canal Trust, officially opened Double Bridge.

In a direct line with Double Bridge was the 'Hunting Bridge' which allowed passage over the River Avon from Lackham. One theory is that this bridge was originally going to be of a similar size to the canal bridge on a road linking two estates, but was never built due to financial restraints. This picture is probably pre-1940.

Lacock Brewery is situated on the hill above the canal and almost certainly used Lacock Wharf near the Bell Inn to tranship their raw materials and finished products, c.1890.

The lock house at Melksham Forest Lock was still inhabited in 1947 when this picture was taken. As with many of these cottages, it shows signs of having at some time in its canal life had an extension on the side, although it still had an outside WC and a well.

The last person to live in the lock cottage until the late 1950s was Bessie Townshend. The lady in this 1947 photo of the rear of the cottage is Dorothy Swanborough, Bessie's daughter, with her husband and children, Brenda and Raymond.

In Melksham, the east side of Lowbourne Bridge still remains today although the rest of it has gone.

The west side of Lowbourne Bridge, *c*.1910.

Looking east towards Lowbourne Bridge, this nicely posed picture from around 1910 clearly shows how quickly the canal became overgrown when regular boat traffic ceased. There is a narrow channel which might indicate that the occasional vessel still fought its way through.

Gallows Footbridge, close to Spa Road, *c.*1900. The name still remains a mystery.

Spa Road Bridge, *c.*1900. The building on the left is Maggs' rope works, and on the other side of the bridge is the Melksham Wharf wharfinger's house.

Spa Road with the bridge over the canal in the distance, *c.*1900. The canal runs east to west (left to right). The wharf was on the right side of the bridge and Maggs' rope works on the left far side.

Left: In 1803 Charles Maggs bought a former cloth mill adjoining Spa Road and used it for making rope, matting and tarpaulins. This Charles Maggs is probably a grandson of the founder. This picture dates from around 1890.

Below: Employees Sam Guley, Alfred Redman and Charles Park inside Maggs' rope works, *c.*1890.

By the 1970s lorries had replaced boats at Melksham Wharf, although many of the buildings still remain. This picture was taken from Spa Road Bridge.

Redevelopment in Melksham has ensured that nothing now remains.

On the way to Semington the canal followed the line of this track, *c.*1960. The large house (known as Semington Dock) belonged to boatbuilder William Large.

This is the boat-builder's shed that was a short distance further down the canal, close to an old public house known as the Railway Tavern. A dry dock was in front of this shed and the canal behind the photographer. *c.*1960.

After passing the farm, the canal ran down towards Semington Junction alongside the road. A sign of the times is that the railway bridge over the waterway has already been removed. The Railway Tavern and the boatbuilders' shed would have been just the other side of the railway bridge, *c*.1960.

As at Abingdon, it is said that the remains of the lock at Semington Junction are buried in the garden of the old toll house, *c*.1960.

A desolate view of a sunken narrowboat, opposite the junction, seen from the bottom lock on the Kennet & Avon Canal at Semington, *c.*1965.

This derelict working boat lies opposite the junction with the Semington lock-keeper's house in the distance, *c.*1965.

Semington Junction, *c.*1900. The spectators are more interested in the local village photographer, Richard Hancock, who they probably all knew, than in the expectation of witnessing traffic on the canal.

ACKNOWLEDGEMENTS

I have not credited individual pictures as in many cases the same image may have come from two (or more) sources. I would like to thank all the following (not in any order of precedence) for their help and encouragement as well as the donation of material: Chris Graebe, Paul Williams, Janet Flanagan, Keith and Maureen Walker, Chris Naish, Ray Denyer, Peter Williams, F.E.J. Burgess, Tony Pratt, Tim Preece, David Banfield, Reg Wilkinson, R.V.G. Brown, Martin Haigh, Martin Boydon, Gloria Loakes, Eric Tull, Neil Rumbol, Barbara Small, G.P. Osbourne, Brian Stovold, John Harrod, Michael Kidley, Liz Drury, Neil Lover, Luke Walker, Gerry Townsend, *Swindon Advertiser*, Swindon Society, Steve Johnson, June Fry, Geof Austin, Geof Newland, Vic Miller, Bob Howlett, Mike Matthews, Anne Sawyer and the many members of WBCT who have offered advice and assistance.

FURTHER INFORMATION

Author's website: http://www.gentle-highway.info
Author's email: dg.small@ukonline.co.uk

The Wilts & Berks Canal Trust,
Spittleborough Farm,
Swindon Road,
Wootton Bassett,
Wiltshire, SN4 8ET

Telephone: 0845 226 8567
Fax: 0845 094 3653
Email: administrator@wbct.org.uk
Website: http://www.wbct.otg.uk

BOOKS:

Small, Doug, *Wilts & Berks Canal*
Dalby, L.J., *The Wilts & Berks Canal*
Hadfield, Charles, *The Canals of South & South East England*
Tull, Eric V., *Canal Days in Swindon*

POSTSCRIPT

As has been mentioned, the Wilts & Berks Canal, including the North Wilts and Calne branches, is currently under active restoration. The length of the canal, around sixty miles, makes this the biggest canal project in the country, and correspondingly increases the number of obstacles to be overcome. The dogged determination of the volunteers of the Wilts & Berks Canal Trust (previously known as the Wilts & Berks Canal Amenity Group) has kept the project moving forward for over three decades. If their enthusiasm should at times tend to wane there soon comes a high spot that rejuvenates them; the start of the twenty-first century has witnessed several such events. Beavans Bridge was totally rebuilt in 2000, and the River Key aqueduct was restored, both with the aid of lottery money. There was the Wiltshire Water Festival at Templars Firs in 2002. The navigable culvert under the Purton road has been completed and 2006 saw the opening of the new Thames 'Jubilee' Junction. Swindon Council is actively promoting the main line of the canal to come back through the town centre to rejoin with the North Wilts branch and developers at Westleaze have built a substantial road bridge over the canal. HRH Camilla, Duchess of Cornwall, became the Patron of the Trust, and in 2009 officially opened the rebuilt 'Double Bridge' near Reybridge. Locks three and four at Seven Locks have been rebuilt and preparatory work has started on locks one and two. A fine new lift bridge has been built above Foxham Top Lock. Chaddington Top Lock was also rebuilt and nearby a huge new spillweir has nearly been completed. The canal between Challow and Childrey has received a great deal of attention with the towpath being almost completely reinstated, much of the canal bed cleared and a stone wharf having been rebuilt. Other projects continue, such as the work at Steppingstone Lane Bridge, the preservation of Latton Basin and its associated structures, Hayes Knoll Lock has been cleared preparatory to rebuilding and work at the three Pewsham locks has begun, whilst in the background Trust members engage with landowners, developers, councils and potential funders to ease the way ahead.

Of course there are holdups and delays, the biggest being in the Abingdon area where the continuing saga of the proposal to build a new reservoir is preventing active restoration until a final decision is made. If it does go ahead, much of the original canal line in the area will be lost and a restored canal will be routed around the reservoir. The Trust remains neutral in its opinion as to what the outcome should be, but is frustrated by the long delay in getting a final decision.

When my first volume of pictures was published in 1999 I did not think it possible that there would ever be enough material for a second book. Fortunately, new pictures have been unearthed. There are still huge gaps, particularly in the lack of images of a working canal. Research into the canal is ongoing; if you can help, please get in touch.

Other titles published by The History Press

Midlands Canals: Memories of the Canal Carriers

ROBERT DAVIES

The men, women and children of all ages that lived and worked on the Inland Waterways experienced a Spartan existence. They would often commence work at 4 or 5 a.m., before shovelling out of the boat nearly 20 tons of coal, boating until well after dark. Many boats contained a whole family that would live, cook and sleep using a tiny cabin at the rear. This superbly researched and illustrated book spans the 1930s to 1960s, a time when transport of goods and materials went through great changes.

978 0 7524 3910 5

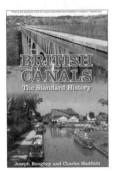

British Canals: The Standard History

JOSEPH BOUGHEY

The first edition of British Canals was published in 1950 and was much admired as a pioneering work in transport history. Joseph Boughey, with the advice of Charles Hadfield, has previously revised and updated the perennially popular material to reflect more recent changes. For this ninth edition, Joseph Boughey discusses the many new discoveries and advances in the world of canals around Britain, inevitably focussing on the twentieth century to a far greater extent than in any previous edition of this book.

978 07524 4667 7

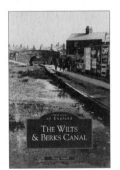

The Wilts & Berks Canal

DOUG SMALL

The Wilts & Berks Canal was opened in 1810 but promoted from 1793. Abandoned in 1914, urban development took its toll on the canal and in some of the country areas it was returned to agricultural use. But the rural nature of this navigation was in many ways its salvation, meaning much of it lay undisturbed. Since 1977 the canal has been under active restoration and is now the biggest project of its type in the country. With over 180 photographs and informative captions, Doug Small portrays this much-loved waterway.

978 07524 1619 9

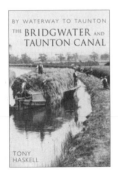

The Bridgwater and Taunton Canal: By Waterway to Taunton

TONY HASKELL

A canal to connect the Bristol and English Channels was envisioned in Somerset at the height of England's 'canal mania' in order to save ships from having to navigate around the hazardous Cornish coast. Sadly this vision was never completed, but the section linking Bridgwater and Taunton opened in 1827. By the First World War it lay it a state of decline until the mid-1990s when, following years of dedication and hard work, craft were once again seen on the restored Bridgwater and Taunton Waterway.

978 0 7524 4267 8

Visit our website and discover thousands of other History Press books.

www.thehistorypress.co.uk

The History Press